JENNN

Who's the TETHER, *Who's the* BALLOON?

outskirts
press

Outskirts Press, Inc.
http://www.outskirtspress.com

Paperback ISBN: 978-1-9772-4596-0

Outskirts Press and the "OP" logo are trademarks belonging to Outskirts Press, Inc.

PRINTED IN THE UNITED STATES OF AMERICA

Contents

Persephone and Demeter

I'll explain to you my dear reader
Were a daughter and mother
Unlike any other
So below is the myth
The heart and the pith
Persephone lived her youth happily, playing with the
Olympian children
But all changed as a young adult … when
Zeus, her father and Hades had struck a deal
And then Persephone was tricked into eating
pomegranate seeds as her meal
Now goddess Demeter's yearlong earthly abundance
would fallow
The depth of her beauty would certainly shallow
So, spring and summer
Persephone unites with her mother
And everything becomes ok
In March, April, June and May
And July, August and part of September
Then the winter-like memories of what happened haunt
as I remember
For my mother was Demeter, pulling me back to life
From the Lord of the Dead who was causing so much strife
It all started with me
Picking narcissus under a tree
With this knowledge, like my mind does winter and spring
I will not succumb to anything

The Red Bow (Nurses put a red bow in my hair when I was born)

As the legend goes
They said "Yup, she's one of those."
Asking my mom what did the red bow signify?
Hmmmm. I'm still trying to find out why...

My youth was good all things considered
My early twenties rough, my brain felt littered
With too much information
On many an occasion
Maybe this was the red (read) bow
That I was battling toe to toe

The red bow in my thirties
Was a doctorate and a marriage
Onto Oswego with my sometimes cultivated carriage
I had some doubt, I won't write about

Forties the same, nothing to write home
Still driving to Oswego. Every faculty meeting a poem

As I turned fifty
A divorce and meeting my life mate
Maybe my little red bow was sealing my fate
Reflecting on all of my chapters in my younger years
I understand now. I can't fight the tears.
Because the little red bow

Was a bit of a prophecy that day
Oh...to make me stronger be that as it may
Yet! Everyone has red bows in their hair
Even if they're not visible, they're still there
The Red Bow
Symbol of what we know
Ties us together
So we may 'red" ily grow.

About the Pandemic by an Academic

Trump's gotten Pence-ive
About the virus being exten-sive
From not being bothered
To being sure
That this pandemic will kill
250,000 or more
C'mon people! He only cares about reelection
That's his motivation for his freestyle word selection
No one can get together and protest
That this is a flippin' cluster of a mess
We are bravely continuing to have a lot less
Hopefully "Summertime" will come, dear Porgy and Bess
To alleviate this incredible MIND-numbing stress

Good Mourning

"Good Mourning!" said the barista at Target
"Good Mourning" I said back, my coffee needs met
My interaction with people is staged
I'm the comic that's dying on the floor feeling caged
I try to make myself smaller, as I am a minicelebrity
I wear specific solid colors that signify MUCH to me!
My inner psyche is bleeding into my outer world
My ability to "understand it all" has completely unfurled
Wow. I was hearing voices, wait I'm ACTUALLY
hearing voices!
People before Corona talked louder, and were closer…
…AND…Didn't give me many choices
But Coronavirus has put an end
To my disassociation, my friend
I'm on the good road, I'm on the mend
The pandemic now not only in my brain
Has led me back to being quite sane

Ma'am I am

When did grocery clerks start calling me Ma'am?
Who the hell do they think I am?
I feel like a spring chicken, a fawn, a foal
How did my face start to take its toll?
The absolute worst is the platform Zoom
Crepy, creepy lines on my neck while chillin' in my room
And furthermore, I don't understand this net generation
Who in twenty years will be deciders of our Nation (OMG)
I'm fifty-five
Vibrant and alive
I think in general I look pretty good
Something I guess I have misunderstood
Because I feel like I'm down for the count on my yoga mat
And the grocery clerk says, "Do you want A BAG with that?"

Dedicated to Professor Tom Yingling

It was the eighties, the scare was AIDS
Our memories of this epidemic now fades
I was an undergrad at Syracuse in English Ed.
I met an English professor, he with balding head
I was smitten
The bug had bitten
He was amazing in class, going above and beyond
I took an independent study, that forged our bond
He'd bring me to dine at the exclusive club for faculty
We'd talk about sleigh rides, his sister and what was
going on with me
I saw him at the mall once, where he gave me a wink
Introduced his partner Art, this made me think
For he studied Hart Crane, and he was an out gay man
But I was his straight, just a girl, ironic biggest fan
We navigated our identities, our attraction wasn't
through touch
My roommate would roll her eyes and say, "Jen, this
really is too much."
I felt that this was the highest form of platonic love
We never talked about anything like this, or "high things
up above".
I found out about his death in a video store
His colleague happened to be there, at the same time,
nothing more
He told me of Tom's death
I felt heavy and out of breath
For the weight of this started to unfurl
Mourning like a woman, no longer a girl

The Reading War

Is a fallacy
To those of us trying to keep normalcy
What it is for you to see
Is a false dichotomy
It is something fabricated
To keep both sides intimidated
If I say I teach phonics sometimes not embedded
I'm wrong and I should've been vetted
If I say comprehension is best overall
The other side wants me to take a fall
The argument keeps us from WHAT WE NEED TO DO
TEACHING STUDENTS WHO NEED READING
SKILLS it's sad but true.
Those philosophies, stances, get in the way
Because the two sides of the coin are here to stay
It's spiraled into "Do you believe in G-d?"
If you don't believe in my side, you're a sell-out, a fraud
It's most important for everyone TO LISTEN WELL
To try to understand what we're all TRYING TO TELL
That the reading war shouldn't be a militant,
evangelical crusade
For we need BOTH so much, that's how we're made
I'm pleading please read Maryanne Wolf's Reader,
Come Home
For those of you who approve or disapprove of this poem

I Gave My Senior Speech

I gave my senior speech on the challenge of nuclear war.
I waited five seconds of silence then applause and roar
I had been scared on that very day
To let myself talk from the heart in that way

I spent some time getting my four degrees
My hometown was a welcoming breeze
I was always a sort of Wandering Jew
Only it was me that I was subject to

I remember being very close to Berrigan Carol
I was her student, ironic she'd wear Old Navy apparel
Am I an activist? more like a canary in a mine of coal
Sometimes the outside pressure hits me to my soul

Tonight, I loved LOVED hearing Rabbi Arthur Waskow
He pulled no punches, his message like POW

Talking about Berrigan Dan
I grew up close to the Oski family clan
That housed and looked after this spectacular man

So, I do wish I could be more "active" than "ist"
Maybe cause I'm not entirely pissed?

I don't have a very loud voice
That's my make up and not a choice
I have my mission

To help with the Native American condition
That is my function
At this particular junction

I'm more think local
Than act global

Freedom is when everyone is free
I have to thee as well as me

A Passover Afternoon

Our 3:00pm Freedom Passover
Is now officially much over
We all met virtually through Zoom
In a square box we all separately loom
We ate the bitter horseradish with the sweet
Bittersweet is how we meet
We talked about our modern plague
It is COVID-19 we were not vague
We told the story of Exodus
Our Freedom Seder, socially just
Matza bread of Freedom on our lips
We recline in our position from our hips
Thank you very much Beth and George
From this seder we march on, peace we forge
As we say at the end
Next year in Jerusalem
But it became next year at a live seder table
Baruch HaShem

My Evolution

I was a new freshman at Brown
My roommate and her mom greeted me with a frown
She said her ancestors "…came from the Mayflower."
"Ellis Island" I quipped and then she became dour

I picked up a book at the Sci Li
I don't even know why
It was about evolution and I started to cry

I went to a place in NH near Greene at nineteen
Here, I was standing at the crime scene
Raw, out in the rain
Feet on the ground, head in the sky…a symbolic evolution
refrain

I picked up a book at the Sci Li
I don't even know why
It was about evolution and I started to cry

I continued on my sojourn
At Syracuse I started to learn
At Oswego now I do teach
I'd like every student to reach

I remember picking up a book at the Sci Li
I don't even know why
It was about evolution and I started to cry

Evolution and its theme
Has continued in my dream
2020 while we look back
My subconscious opens up a crack

I remember picking up a book at the Sci Li
I don't even know why
It was about evolution and I started to cry

During this Corona time, I see many connections
In all parts and parts of sections
Of what is meant to be
My epiphany

Now I know why I picked up a book at the Sci Li
It's about evolution!
I give a big sigh

Mom and Dad

I rarely talk about my Dad
Or the life that he had
Growing up, Mom was more hypomanic
Dad more depressed, but both prone to panic
To many, Mom was always in a good mood
Dad was more and more prone to brood
I have the luxury of inheriting both
Sunshine and rain, from their seedling to even more growth
I was once called a "flower of humanity"
If I were a flower, a hydrangea I'd be
Bursting blue/purple filled with flowery grace
Yet my Dad and his dark and silent place
And my Mom in her Hallelujah light
This all stems from my parents' plight
As well as their unsinkable might

My Folly with Grandma Molly

A CEO she should have been
She was my grandma, my next of next of kin
I thought she never really liked me at all
She tried to bribe me at the mall
I was seven and we were arguing
About what, I don't remember, but it was "a thing"

She took her wallet out and gave me a five-dollar bill
I said to her "You can't buy me" as I sat there still
So, every year after that on my birthday
I got a tree from Israel rather than a monetary gift tou-che
Haven't really thought about it, until today

For, I recently received two more trees as a wedding gift
Years later this really helped to repair the grandma rift
As the new trees are saplings and some older are
forty-eight
I guess it's not too late
For the trees to qualify
As a way to "Mollify"

SAD SADNERIO

What if Trump gets reelected?
What if the hatred goes viral...yet also selected?
Many intellectuals will be on more meds
 Abilify and anti-depressants because of the feds
Shouldn't say, but the movement is very much rural
I think it's about basic accrual

In the news I saw a protest in Michigan
In cars with masks, women and many a man
So, they're protesting for the economy, the opening of stores
But wearing the virus combat uniform in scores!

OMG. What the FUTS?
Are they absolutely NUTS?!
Is this because they are in the rut of their RUTS?
We have to do something symbolic
In order to make this less vitriolic
We may be out of the woods
By this November
I'll be voting for Biden who's upfront and center

I may be wearing my mask that day
To signifying the metaphoric virus
Getting in our way
By opening the marketplace too soon
Trump's aiming for an economic boon
Which may be America's ruin
So sad

So bad
So mad
So had
Not glad
A tad rad
What a cad

Many a Cat- Is Where I'm At

Mom would be walking
Hands with hot tea and coffee…talking
Tina would kamikaze bite
Mom's ass to Tina's delight
Tina was a genius who retrieved fresh green beans
She typically slinked behind the couch and scenes
naughtynaughtynaughtynaugthy…say it fast
Sounds like "naughty" or "Tina" first syllable and last

Then there was our cat Nori
Who was a completely different story
Nice, furry, warm
Mom only took HER to the basement
when there was a storm
Then Nermal entered my life
He would hiss with all his angsty strife
Beautiful Maine-Coon
Unfortunately, he went too soon

Minnie was a small grey
Who always made Ed's day
I cried and cried
Because it wasn't only she that died
We go to the kitty cat café
A place where you and cats can play
Peter's allergic, antihistamine he takes
When I want to adopt he puts on the brakes

Now and then we go on a kitty walk
There's the neighborhood Andy and Gary; they meow
talk
I have cat everything
That takes out the sting
Because I'll confess
I am a mess
About the joys these animals bring

Design is a Sign

I love to go to Corning Museum of Glass
The "hot shop" creations are always kick-ass

I also love designer Anna Sui
I could wear her clothes indefinitely

Mass MOCA is my favorite museum
Their installations bold and heavy, you should see'um

I love LOVE the inherent design in a book
Tommy Orange's <u>There, There</u> where there's a particular
hook

So what does all of this mean?
Except that each is a part of an artistic "scene"

Can we make mass generalizations?
About these massive creations?

For sure
I see that all mediums attempt to evoke...
In each case, something inside of them and beautiful
awoke
All of these high wire design acts fearless go for broke
Amazing the creative fires they stoke

Zoom distorts one's face

It does not do it grace
I look like the mug shot of Nick Nolte (google)
And have a sallow neck looking like poutry

My hair, the consistency of string
But I want to break out and sing:

'What do I really look like in this state?"
My self-esteem is in the basement not great
I ask my sheepish shipmate

He says don't pay attention to Zoom
Try to block it, leave the chat room

I try to be forgiving and kind
I'm going out of my harebrained mind

I guess I am humbled
"I say" like I mumbled

"Why is a salon that's open so hard to find?"

Noblesse Oblige Prestige

During the era I went to Brown
I chatted with the Prince of Jordan, in line for the crown
And later in the early era of Ronald Reagan
I found myself in an arena sitting next to Carl Sagan
I was lucky enough to sit
Near these people of fame and wit
Billie Jean says "Pressure is a privilege"
And I continue to make my pilgrimage
To make music and tennis accessible: played and seen
To approaching Shakespeare… you now know what I mean
"Tennis balls my liege" from Henry the 5th
The royals anointed by G-d may be one big myth
Wide-awake-ness said philosopher Maxine Greene
Is our reaction to aesthetics, but what does this mean?
Appreciating art in any form
Having a moving experience not forlorn
This could be how the soul, mind spirit is reborn
Oh, here I go tooting my fox horn
Even my poems have endings that rhyme
Easy to read (never highbrow) most of the time
It sounds a little snooty, noblesse oblige
Yet, I'm a conduit between down to earth and prestige
We daily walk to what we call "Swiss street"
The chalets of Ithaca are on our beat
So perhaps I'm being a Swiss in the US
Promoting a beautiful vision I confess
Yodeling through the pastures fair
Trying not to put on an air
Because I really care
And I try to do as others I dare

We Planned Our Honeymoon

We planned our honeymoon in New York City
Instead I walk to Wegman's, masked, not so pretty
I'm trapped, it's cold and snow just was here
Will we be doing this I fear, for the next calendar year?
I hear my husband's keyboard playing notes
His music class and the undergrads, he kindly dotes
He is so sweet in a Mr. Roger's voice
Giving voluntary zoom meetings as a choice
In my grad class we raucously laugh
I kid them and make many a gaffe
We have bonded, we have fun
Can't believe the semester is almost done
Peter and I have a different style
He super nice, me with a little guile
So we do approach our classes differently
It's who we are...he and me

Having a party of one

Looking at my CD's this morning, it's just begun
Oh, here to Syracuse we go
Memories flow
And in my car I do upper body freestyle and do si do
Kenny Loggins, Howard Jones, the Doobie Bro's
Expressin' it from head to toes
I'm pretty sure I'm inspired
Perhaps I'm kind of in it…mired
I sing and cry sometimes, it's episodic
The music feels so darn hypnotic
"I feel for you" sings Chaka Khan
With my diet coke mic I sing on and on
My concert ends with Carey, Mariah
Encore Madonna "Vogue" I'm on fy-a
I exit the car with my sunglasses
Leaving my fans the "M&M wrappers" en masses
Then it's back to reality
Peter, what it is it like to live with such a celebrity?

Me and Peter

Me and Peter, like rhyme and meter
First met in Skaneateles Bakery
And walked along the lakery
It was home at first sight
I sealed the deal with a menorah to light
Next day was his day of birth
He invited me to share in the mirth
I stopped at his Ithaca house
Quiet as a mouse
Didn't know I was to be his spouse

Flash forward to 2019
At a castle was the scene
We married there
And carried there
Our vivid hope and dream

Six months later I'm living on Wood Street
Where on that fateful second date we did meet
Regards to "The Odd Couple" Peter is Felix and I am
Oscar
He feet on the ground, me in a flying saucer

I'm trying to be neat
Not an easy feat
Peter's pretty patient with all my mess
Peter's meter becomes stressed and unstressed
For we are living this poetry
I love him and he loves me

Mavericks, Trailblazers, Artistes

Excellence at the very leasts
I'm attracted to the complicated
I don't have time for the over, overrated
I'm now a fan of glassblowing!
A risky art that keeps growing
And it's conceptual, depends on knowing
There is a show called "Blown Away"
"Contestants" compete for a shot to all the way stay
It's so interesting how they think
They are dangerous to the brink
I tried once to blow glass
I fell right on my ass
I had a burn
So, I could not return
It was a brief sojourn
Though I did learn
The courage it must take
To perhaps get that one big break
Be famous in this medium
Having to earn your way through the tedium
(in the shape of a glass goblet)

Monkeying Around

When I was five…and very alive
I was in a psychological study
That I now feel was a bit muddy
The dissertation was about maternal attachment
And how the mother was able to patch and it meant

That I was left in a room with my mom
And there I felt pretty calm
Then introduced was a terrifying electronic monkey with red flashing eyes,
No lies!
I started crying, that thing I did despise

Mom was supposed to comfort me
I just hid behind her skirt, never to come out and see
I was the ONLY ONE that reacted that way
To this grad student's utter dismay

So, this Doc student thought he had marred me for life
But then he in turn AGAIN added to my strife!
I was outside in our yard, playing under a tree
When the familiar Doc student greeted me

He slowly unwrapped the box with the scary creature
It was lying in repose with no lit electronic feature

I said, "You take your monkey and GO AWAY."
I think I ruined his research that day
But setting limits as a five-year old was very much o.k.

Becoming a Teacher!

Why do you want to teach?
If you say because of summers off
I will scoff
If you say because of the shortened day
That's not o.k.

But if you say it's to make a difference
Because there's so much indifference
If you want to be a role model
And you don't want to coddle

If you have the right combination
Of brains, patience and justice education
You probably will do well
Though you'll have to pay your dues, do tell

A teacher
Is a reacher
Has a kindness feature
But is not a preacher

Being a teacher these days is tough
With all the assessing that makes it rough

But if this has been a dream to become one
Keep calm, carry on, but you never will be done or have
all battles won

How I Write my Poems

Wherever I do roam
Daily I think of a poem!

Sometimes zany, sometimes sweet
Typically, they have a certain beat
It's no small feat
Because none of the topics repeat
Basic qualifications they meet

A particular cadence, a bit of rhyme
That are the result of a specific time
I recall in my life
At times fun, at times strife
I have to wrack my brain
Observing pleasure, reserving pain

Making sure my writing
Hasn't a topic biting
So this is a poem that is reflective
Today it is elective

Meaning you can read the rest if you want to
It's only a personal point of view
Of me through the eyes of you

I'm done!
Toodle-e-do

ZOOMAPHOBIA

Being on Zoom
Is our doom
No one knows how to chat room!!
Our department meeting the other day
Was constantly interrupted to people's dismay

Folks were conversing, oblivious to mute
If it wasn't a little tragic, it would be a hoot

A couple of people would say, "I so move"
A couple of others would second, "I approve"

It was like watching a movie by Christopher Guest
OMG! Total mayhem! To myself, I confessed

After two arduous hours it was time to end our meeting
We shut our boxes down and finally got out of our seating

I thought tenderly, this faculty is so damn loveable
I want to give them each a virtual huggable

It's a sad predicament we are in
But we are doing our best not to give in

Zoom or no zoom, we will survive
Although amusing, these faculty meetings keep me alive.

Visiting Andy the Cat!

We walk in Ithaca every night
There are some signposts in our sight
Down South Albany, right at Court Street where we
have seen
The star, Maine Coon with tabby looking out the
window screen

On the window a bit of masking tape is designed
To tell us his name, "Andy", a sort of makeshift sign
We step closer, look deep in his eyes
He's probably thinking, "What's up with you guys?"

The tenderness that Peter has for this cat
Makes me think he'd be a good dad and all that
We can't have children, but we could be parents to whom
we teach
We are in that age range, and not so out of reach

So, cats, students, our friends, each other we care
We kindheartedly treat them as we are truly aware

So, if Andy's happens to be in the window it's our little treat
Andy we are so happy, thank you, that's no little feat

Bawler Hat

In Jamesville, at a tavern, I met my friend
My first marriage was at, the bitter end
We talked and talked, and talked some more
About my former folklore
I had the hat you gave me
It was a Charlie Chaplinesque bowler hat for all to see
As our meal continued
I felt imbued
to express my discomfort and need
About the divorce deed
You asked how I knew it was love
I couldn't answer or see any signs from above
I only cried and cried and took off the bowler hat
And you said I guess there are no words that can explain
that
From now on my hat took on a new meaning
It was now a "bawler hat" at my seating
It was a sad phase of life
Which had a lot of strife
Years have now passed on
My anger, depression have gone
I was able to move on
And carry the lessons I could
For me it is now understood
My bawler hat has returned to being a bowler hat
That's now where it's at
A mere a memory of the whole thing that is cast
In the past

To the Moms

It's Mother's Day today
Hip Hip Hooray!
To all of you moms I salute
And I have been following suit
Because of the pandemic
I'm less of a hardened academic
During these times I've tried to keep calm
More gentle, more like a mom

The less and less I complain

About my maladies when I sign up for yet another Meal
Train
It's insane
How now I'm in my fifties and more people are in
exponential pain
It's harder to bounce back
From any physical or mental attack
He was sixty when he died
I was at the time twenty-five
I was teaching high school English at Manlius Pebble Hill
We were longing for a magic pill
Now sixty seems young to me
I'm almost fifty-six for all to see
I count many a blessing
At this game where we are guessing
But it also makes me hate
I wonder, "Who's in control our fate?"
In cases where it is too late

The Odyssey

Hey! I found my literary home
This will be the theme of this poem
For the sirens scream often on Green Street
I was lured by the sound that only I could hear
And...my skipping feet
The business is independent and so full of lore
It is called the Odyssey Bookstore
The aesthetic
Is prophetic
Down in the lower part of the edifice
I stood on the bottom step precipice
Dare I go in but lose myself?
Will it be detrimental to my fiscal health?
Circe must live in this space
For I am totally giddy about this place
All are welcome here
No one marginalized/has fear
I'm excited about this store
The nooks of books galore
There's even more
Than just one "novel" experience
And it calls for many a reappearance!

Today is poem number fifty-four

Hard to believe I have created all of this folklore!
I am wondering what is next in store
And I do not want to bore you with my poetic score

In my poems I have talked about my inner and outer
landscape
The sad, the happy, my grand escape can leave mouths
agape

What does it take to write each poem?
Wishing they will live in a tome

When I'm writing I often go back to the event
In a dispassionate way, so I am not spent

I craft the poems with rhyme and reason
A little literary allusion here, imagery there,
primed and seasoned

When the poem is fully cooked, I will know when
Then I'll add more spice again and again
I find this to be my happy medium
Hopefully, you will enjoy these poems (without the
tedium)

Switzerland

I went to Switzerland after my sophomore year at Brown
I lived in Rances, a pretty little town
I had to tend to thousands of chickens inside a facility
I was paid by the hour, I embodied "utility"
I would run the Suchet mountain, eight miles uphill
Best shape of my life, I fit the bill
There was a chalet restaurant on the top
That serves songs, fondue and beer where I loved to stop
I had to learn the language and specific dialect fast
I was ambassador, questions about America I was asked
We worked during the day, sometimes harvesting
beets in the morn
I even witnessed a calf being born
I am a Swiss citizen, a matter of fact
Through my mom, it was our silent pact
My dream was always to go there and teach
But I've married an American, so that's out of reach
So, when I'm in New York, I buy a special watch
That's made in Switzerland, it's called a Swatch
Also, Peter and I make raclette a type of cheese dish
With paprika and cornichons really delish
I wonder thirty-five years later how things are going
Is the walking up the cows to pasture still an event
worth knowing?
Federer, cheese, watches, chocolate, neutrality, on-
time trains
A distant, yet beautiful memory still remains

Because of this, I've changed

Priorities rearranged

Our outing, Wegman's, we go once a week
I wear my mask, muffled sounds I speak
NOW this is for the long haul
I guess "Before you walk, you must crawl"

We are visiting Peter's parents tonight
We are making everything safe: gloves, masks on tight
Thai food is going to be the delight
Can't wait to see them! and have a quick bite

I wish I could play tennis again, my love: doubles
But singles is the game that will grant you no troubles

Another passion of mine
Is fashion design

But NOW it's only sweatshirts and jeans
For me, quite a change of scenes

I'm a hugger but no hugs, introductions now formal
We have to adapt to the (sick of the phrase) "new normal"

Wegman's is our big outing

Wegman's is our big outing of the week
We go Sunday morning, not at the peak
It's surreal, like a Disney movie
Going in, getting carts, sanitizing hands, so groove-y
I always go to the same exact aisles
Nothing differs each week, everything's the same styles
But we walk for what seems seven miles
And it's hard to tell if shoppers have smiles
I buy my citrus: oranges and grapefruits
I pick them by hand, only the beauts
The music here is upbeat, so different from the
"organic" mood
Wham! Whitney Houston, the eighties! "Pshaw" I brood
I slice into the aisle of bread
Oh! Someone is too close, I feel the dread
She says, "I'm sorry, I'm in your way"
I move my cart sheepishly saying, "Oh, It's ok"
Shopping all done, we walk to the car
Emotionally and literally spent, we are
Maybe purgatory or a little bit of hell?
Dunno. Just putting on my mask, and using Purell

Nermal

Nermal's name was chosen in my class
Of summer school students at Syracuse in masse
The final suggestion "Nermal!" came from a guy who
did crew
I showed the kitten's picture that they did view
My professors said this was the ultimate in being
student centered
But I felt it was the right thing, no matter how I'd
been mentored
Nermal grew into a grand nineteen-pound Maine Coon
His high squeaky meow was incredibly fine tuned
He used to have a problem with men
But if you scratched his back tail a certain way he would
hiss and purr and then
The kid that I tutored, Nermal was the main attraction
Even I wasn't getting such a friendly reaction
But then Nermal passed after tutoring during that week
Not sure what to tell the kid who I thought would
completely freak
But this third grader brought a gift to share with me
Faux-Nermal the stuffed animal cat for everyone to see!
I'm looking at Faux-Nermal now he's changed his location
He sits near Ithaca cat at his own station
For I will always have memories of Nermal the cat
Especially when his eyes sat on a mouse or a rat
He merely scanned the rodent in view
Never doing anything but sitting there, nothing new
His instincts were not cat-like more like Buddhist-Zen

He could care what crossed his path, but peeping a little
"Amen"
Nermal, oh Nermal, you were such a fine gent
I still mourn you now that you're heaven-sent

Up on Schitt's Creek

I'm finding all of my friends
Are watching Schitt's Creek to see how it ends
It is a show on Netflix
That is also our nightly fix
Peter and I watch about three episodes per night
The acting is a pure delight
There are three related Levy's in the show
Father Eugene, son Daniel, sister Sarah all in a row
The absolute best is a character played by Daniel
named David
He plays an eyerolling pansexual, affected, he is my fave-kid
It is a way to escape the pandemic
We love the fake town; it's a laugh epidemic
We don't know wife Moira's pedigree or place of origin
Her accent so weird, she seems to need some more of gin
So, while we are up on our Schitt's Creek
We can forget our days of the week
And sneak a peek
At a quirky family's time to freak

The Weighty Conclusion to my Herstory

Go Healthy, NOT Skinny

During my high school senior year
I weighed one hundred seven pounds, I fear
I wanted to be less curvy, more like a narrow straight pole
I was a bit nervy, trying to control
Flash forward: my weight fluctuates
Not a lot, but my fate punctuates
On every time I get on the scale
There is no magic, what the hayle?
On good days I top the scales at one hundred thirty-four
On bad days, I just try to ignore
I've never been bulimic, but a bit too close to anorexic
I have a mean chocolate habit I'd also like to kick
Do I love my body? I'm trying a détente or truce
I walk for miles, I play tennis, I give it lots of use
So, I hope during the pandemic, I relax my weighty rules
Leave it to Vogue, Shape, Glamour, etc. for trying to
make us fools
The pics of celebs, remember Faustian bargain! They are
skinny, yes, but get paid
To be at an unhealthy body weight they so called "have
it made"
At 5% body fat, people start to fade!
There are way too many corpse casualties, I'm afraid
Your body has a set point it typically hovers near
So have a healthy diet, add cream cheese and bagel, schmear!
Be moderate, drink water, once in a while a treat or two
For remember my dear friends, you only have once to
being you!

At college, new knowledge

Reading <u>The Bell Jar</u>
Sylvia Plath's memoir
Took me aback
Had a little panic attack
"The Many Perceptions of Mental Illness" a Brown course
I would relate to it later, as a matter of force
I was planning on majoring in psychology
I took a course in personality theory
But I was not connecting well to my peers
It would be a matter of years
I was put on a regimen
So, that I was scheduled then
In my forties and fifties, I broke free and found more
happiness
My life was now, mostly full of zest
I'm calm, mindful, fully collected
Which is how I stay fully connected
I'm now on my game
The same, from before it came

Memories or What a Wooper!

Vegetables, Flowers and a Rose
Creating gardens from what she knows
Mom won a rose competition and kudos she received
She attached the first-place ribbon to her housecoat sleeve
We used to make fun of her accent, Swiss
She had difficulty at the drive thru, saying Wooper for
Whopper I reminisce
Puppet shows during red lights through the sunroof of
the VW rabbit
We could be playfully acting, it would be our habit
Chardonnays for lunch she was a self-procliamed bonne
vivante
She engaged in life, didn't have a want
For we could be kids
That followed and did not do forbids
Mom doing cartwheels on the lawn
Always around when called upon
Remembering all this takes me back
Hey, I'd like a Wooper, not a Big Mac

Fashion is my Passion

I was just in my quarters, the attic
I have my four racks of clothes if I'm erratic
My "uniforms" are usually full of whimsy
A library skirt, music appliques, bunny tights, all elegant
not flimsy
I don't have a huge personality full of action
But sometimes what I wear causes a reaction
Other days I feel like blending in
Yet sometimes I act like my vivacious twin
A dress golden yellow, a vintage Madonna tee
"Who's that girl?" Well, that she is me
I'm turning fifty-six June twenty-first
I'm getting close to aging out, that feeling is the worst
But, Iris Apfel is an amazing grande dame of fashion
Ninety-eight years old and still full of passion
I have to say, why do I care?
Because it's my signature, like some tattoos or pink hair
Well, I certainly won't go THAT far
In my personal movie, Jen the mini celeb, little star

My Birthday

Is about two weeks away
No parties, fanfare, celebration
Well, look what's going on with the Nation
Trump is hunkered down
In a bunker he has found
We still have Corona
Which we are prone-uhh
I think this Nation is lost
Without strong, coherent leadership at great cost
People going stir crazy
In their house
Taking drives and drag racing they carouse
We HAVE to in November vote Biden
We have to take a strong side then!
'Cause this shit has to be going down
With all this layered stuff going around
So please for my birthday just vote
So we don't have to remain in this this hole-ridden boat

Peter and I live in the same house

My station is the main floor, he is the "upstairs mouse"
I sleep on the couch
A deviated septum makes me a grouch
I can't seem to breathe in the upstairs bed
My nose stuffs up instead
But we are getting along amazingly well
We rarely get into a tiff or a bad spell
All of my clothes are in the attic
About four racks ~ he is in a slight panic
But he keeps his anxiety to a minimum
Though it seems with my stuff we need an extra
condominium
The kitchen light I leave on in the morn
He wants to get a light timer, about this he's forlorn
We eat dinner together, he eats kippers and sardines
I just have Amy's dinners or Lean Cuisines
But even though our respective habits drive us crazy
We are able to delve into our work, can't call us lazy
For Peter is my husband, my soul mate
Kippers and all, he is still great

Goodbye to the Rabbi

This morning we said goodbye
To our esteemed Rabbi
No one can compare
To his strength, compassion and care
Now we have a leadership lay
And I guess this is o.k.
We want someone articulate and strong
Who doesn't mince opinions, even though some feel
these opinions are wrong
We want someone who will fight
Injustice, hate, our plight
For we are better because of he
And all that we are committed to see
We cried at the service's end
A rabbi and a friend

Barnes is Noble

Barnes and Noble has opened its door
Everything in there is pristine galore
We have to sanitize our hands, at a station, Purell
To avoid the COVID19 pandemic hell
Only a few of the customers can go in at a time
Watched by the staff like their witnessing a crime
It seems so eerie
What if I have a query?
Like can I go to the bathroom?
Or is this place the Temple of Doom?
I want to get an iced coffee with a caramel shot
The café is closed I can't sit with what I've bought
I look at the mysteries on the bookcases
The tables of books are set out more than a few paces
Even I recognize the masked face of the purple haired girl
She recognizes me I think by her eye whirl
My eyes smile at her, such a good YA bookseller
But now she seems like she's behind glass, like a bank
teller
It's a bit depressing going to these stores
Without the hubbub of people on the sales floors
No people watching or working online seated in the café
No time for work or even time to meet friends and play
I wish everything was back to OK
I guess we'll have to go through this day to day
But not for much longer, I pray

My clothing is a spectacle

I find my taste delectable
I have all kinds of dramatic shoes
They look like pencils, donuts, even suede blues
My skirts have libraries, telephones, cats
The older I get, the wear it's ats
For I'm a literacy professor and I wear stories in this way
I was much more conservative, back in the day
Only Ann Taylor blue or black suits I wore
Trying to look older, trying to be a bore
Then after awhile, I started to be kitschy and cute
The clothes speaking volumes, I needed to put it on mute
So I wear one special item, only one of whimsy
And I make sure it's nicely tailored not flimsy
My bags are another thing altogether
Toasters, phones, LP records no matter the weather
For I'm turning fifty-six June twenty-first
I need to keep rockin' until the seams burst!

A Nuclear Foreboding

At high school graduation I was selected to speak
For I was kinda cool, but also a geek
I spoke about the challenges that we face
Surprise! It was about the nuclear arms race
I tried to positively spin
The fact that the world could pull together and win
Some parents stopped me and thanked me for a job
well-done
Then the summer between high school and college was
overdone
Perhaps it was the beginning of the bomb inside
I was about to embark on a bumpy ride
Time was ticking away, and I knew I couldn't stay
I took a couple of years away
Motivated and more mature
Teaching was my calling; it was part of my cure
So, I tell my students and young adults – go back when
you're ready
Go back when your equilibrium is steady
And don't worry what people say
You'll go through some hoops be that as it may
And ultimately you'll learn and you'll be okay

I'm on poem number eighty-four

I'm happy with my verses galore
I just wish my feet weren't so sore
From walking downtown to other locations some more
I went into a few shops on the Ithaca Commons
Just to look rather than cause any problems!
The restaurants are now serving outside
Table after table with spaces six feet wide
I'd love a hotdog from vendor Lou
For special occasions for this non-kosher Jew
It is so hot, at least ninety degrees
But I do like this better than the cold winter freeze
Pollen around makes me terribly sneeze
At least there is a bit of a breeze
So, I'm basically every day in Tompkins County
Will go to Farmer's Market Saturday for veggie and
fruit bounty
I can now say I'm an Ithaca Native 'cause I'm here full-time
I'm here for the duration, I support Ithaca's excellence.
It's prime.

A Continuation of the Poem from Yesterday

I went downtown today
To have that hotdog, from Lou, if I may
Then I went to Petrune, A cool vintage clothing store
And talked to the owner, she's moving next door
She was very upbeat, friendly and we chat
She spoke about the promise of new beginnings, but
also where we're at
For I was the only one in the shop
I had to ring a bell, enter with mask, put sanitizer on
my hand's top
I told her a bit about myself and how I'm newly full-
time in this town
She made my day by being earth to down
I've been thinking that I have a lot of time
To do what I want to do and fit in my daily rhyme
It is important to me to get in my daily walks
I walk downtown a bit and talk my daily talks
COVID is a drag but I think there is a silver lining
It gives us time to converse, a way of shining
So, I support small business, I go to Ithaca Coffee Co.
nearly every morn
I'm happy to be part of this fabric, my life reborn

Shopping at Co-op Green Star

COVID says no salad bar
Seems kind of a corporate vibe
So sleek the aisles they come alive
It is about three sizes bigger than the old market
The lot is huge ~ places to park it
But the new shop seems to exhale some of its former soul
What used to be more intimate space is now on a
corporate kind of roll
I like the variety of the things to buy
You can get almost all that you wish, even different kinds
of rye
Seems much more like Whole Foods
If you're in that kind of moods
I have to give the store some props
Though they still believe in Co-ops
Where people have to belong and be a member
Then they get dividends in terms of tender
So, I may just belong
Even as I sing this blues song
Cause I hope many Ithaca people go
To get their groceries and cup of joe

It's my birthday week

Started today, so to speak
I'm celebrating every day until this coming Sunday
When I share my birthday with Father's Day what a fun day
Same Sunday happened when I was born, a girl not a boy
I was given a lamp not a stuffed animal or toy
My mother said it was because I was the light
Of dad's world, shining big and so bright
I recall sitting in a big blue stuffed chair
Doing my homework in back of dad sitting there
We played monopoly against my mom and brother
Dad and I so competitive against "the other"
He used to play tennis with his doctor friends
I still play tennis, similarity never ends
I'm Dr. Kagan, will not change my name
Maybe I'll live up to "the original's" fame
For I hope to live in a way that honors my dad
He never witnessed me growing older, but I wish he had

Today I went to Cayuga Nails

They were so careful, it seemed "off the rails"
I could not pick up a type of polish
Considered a mortal sin, they would me, demolish
There were shields and glass barriers everywhere
They have thought of everything, I felt good in their care
My feet were sloughed off, so much residue
Three months of walking, now I had a vivid view
My fingers got polished clear
I didn't want to take off hardened gel nails, what a fear
So, I feel like Dorothy, the scarecrow, lion and tinman
When they got all coiffed in Wizard of Oz, so I can
Next get my hair done
Not sure if I want to go short, or have a long run
My birthday week is getting fun!
But I have so much to do besides my day of birth
I'd like to laugh and experience more mirth
But I have a lot of work to complete
So I have to get beyond my lovely feet

Doc School

I decided to get my Ph.D.
It was the next step, to me being me
I toiled and toiled getting the degree
But no one ever said it was free
I had a graduate assistantship
Teaching "College Learning Strategies" wasn't I hip
I taught study skills to athletes and more
To kids on academic probation where I evened the score
There was a single mom who desperately needed childcare
So I looked after her ten-month year-old son because I
wanted to be fair
I took him in stroller to T.G.I.F. Fridays
Never lunched with a ten-month old, I was amazed
Then there was a study where I tutored grades second
and third
Some of the best techniques that I have ever heard
Still though working on my dissertation
Like of marathon duration
On to the defense
It was pleasant, cordial, made sense
Now I am a Dr. Jen
Following in the footsteps of a Kagan
Twenty years since, are passing this November
It's kind of a blur but some things I do remember
That people – profs, grad students, secretaries were
genuinely kind
That sometimes I stretched my mind
But I will always move forward with the notion
That I would remember my grad experience with devotion

Doug's Fishfry

For my birthday we are going to Doug's
It's a fishfry that sells hotdogs…my drugs
I'm so looking forward to my garden of eatin'
We have to go outdoors for our seatin'

I load the dog with mustard and relish
People look at my creation and they're jealish
Add a little baked beans and some coleslaw
Just like it was made by my Maw

Downward dog, the bites go south
All the coney and bun starts from my mouth
I always agonize
If I should get the fries

So, it's unhealthy but it's frankfurter heaven
Out of a score of ten, I give it an eleven
So awesome is Doug's in Cortland here
And my memories of dining there that I hold dear

HAPPY BIRTHDAY MARION!

The 1,000Watt smile
The understated style
Everything in her power flourishes
From the animals to plants she nourishes
By day she manages Drumlins Tennis Club
Much because of her, it is a tennis HUB
Her office shows off her decorative flair
No matter the hour, Oy, she's almost always there!
Is Marion almost too good to be true?
She's of strong Polish stock and has a healthy point of view
She gives great care and advice to her friends
Going that extra mile that never ends
This past October my Honor Maid
Calming me as my nerves were a tad frayed
She looks so good, we are apart four years
Everyone guesses four years YOUNGER as we are
incredible peers
I don't know how she does it, but she does it with love
And her strong faith in G-d up above
We were born on the same day
And we are different but alike in a similar way
I call her Merry Onion, like Marion, a simple word play
Always a sunny disposition, one to make your day
So, what the heck is wrong with this awesome human being?
There is nothing wrong, as far as I am seeing
She has a calling, and is called Marion ~ she's tall
She's motivated by a distinctive clarion call

Corona, Bemoana

Now the Corona Virus is diminishing its scare
But the reality is still there
Don't let up!
With your mask get-up!
States are loosening the rules
And there are a lot of fools
Who could care less about contracting
That's why they are carelessly interacting
Cuomo says "We are New York tough"
Yet, that just isn't enough
On a recent walk at Green Lakes
I saw behavior that was high stakes
It was like an episode of Twilight Zone
The only one with a mask was me, and I was literally all alone
According to Trump he will again make America great
But there were few crowds at his rallies that took this bait
The maskless man who constantly tweets and spews
Isn't getting too many good reviews
So, we talk about silver lining
It's not only that we now have fine dining
People are uprising
And it's needed yet somewhat surprising
From the government we are not taking our cues
To rally is what some choose
To express their point of views
I'm heartened that there is such a move
'Cause this has catapulted a groove for people to prove
That we face inequities all the time
And we are finally getting to the root of our crime

Who's the Tether? Who's the Balloon?

My dad was straight forward, a doctor, a tether
He worried about everything, including the weather
He was grounded in science and thought less about the arts
He knew about medicine and all of its distinctive parts
My mom, a balloon, loose and up high
Floating above in her bright blue sky
Knew she needed a tether to keep her down to earth
She often was very full of joy and full of mirth
So, dad and mom reached an agreement soon
That dad was the tether and mom the balloon
Peter and I share the tether and balloon responsibilities as well
For we have different abilities, that I'm about to tell
I am education - literacy while he is music theory
Sometimes both exhausted that we get "job weary"
When I stop making sense tether Peter brings me back
He understands me and my mind that's on the attack
I think I add some balloonish levity
Which contributes to our relationship longevity
He has a problem with me making a mess
It causes him much profound distress
I have a problem that he's so tidy
It gets to the point of religious piety
I hope that we both can heal-ium
From each of our respective delirium
But it's also nice that we are not like the other
Just like my dad who loved my mother
For whom is without a little strife?
Honestly, Peter and I make a nice and comfortable life

The Way to Becoming Jenny

Finished <u>The Way to Becoming Yaelle</u> (Ya-el)
It was an interesting Jewish tale
About a girl who visits Israel and is transformed
Her "Jewishness" is basically reborn
I can relate to her becoming more of a Jew
Because from my point of view
I'm now one that is practicing too
Our wedding performed by a Cantor
During the ceremony we fell into a back and forth banter
The Hebrew meaning so much more
It rattled and shook me to my core
Peter and I are leading service this Friday night
I'm adding poems that shine the light
On Jews and human's common plight
At these services I feel part of a bigger whole
It is in community where I play a role
Never did I think I'd go back to where I began
Now I say, "I'm a Jew" and take more of a stand
And perhaps I, like Yaelle, I will visit the promise land
How grand

How to be an Ally

I've been playing tennis for about fifty years
It has brought me much joy among my peers
I belong to Drumlins Tennis Club, I go on many occasion
Not only do I play, but I teach tennis at the Onondaga
Nation
One story of mine, leaps out at me
About including minorities, the oppressed and
LGBT(QIA)
For several years I brought poets to the Onondaga Nation
School
The initiative was pretty cool
They were getting their M.F.A.
They both taught creative writing to the fifth and sixth
grade and they are gay
They taught rhyme, rhythm, and Haiku
They were talented and funny, like me and you!
But when they taught the kids how to brainstorm and
write
A character sketch's ideas were on the board along with
his plight
The kids decided they wanted their character to be gay
It was an homage to these poets, and it was totally o.k.
After this idea, the three of us did nod
But the host teacher was uncomfortable and said an
almost inaudible "Oh God".
The writers and the ally
Let out a collective sigh
We said, "Whatever you kids want"

There was much warmth in the room and not even one
taunt
I wanted to tell the story
About a success, or perhaps a glory
Remembering my all-time favorite professor
And my rainbow wearing hairdresser
From a nephew, now a niece
To my gay friend who is police
We have to be vocal right now, right here
For anyone who identifies queer
For I'm an ally straight
And my gay friends I love like a doubles teammate

Lunch at Panera Bread

Where we met and where we were fed
My friend was my college roommate
We caught up on our lives as we ate
About two years ago she had surgery
It was not elective, it was emergency
She's come back from the brink
A miracle! that's what I think
When I think about her, as a writer
I describe her strength as amazing, she's a fighter
We've grown up a lot since our days at S.U.
She's now a wonderful teacher with a sensitive, street-
wise point of view
She cares much, wears her heart on her sleeve
Those kids that she inspires, she makes them truly believe
For now, I truly appreciate my friend
She's got my back, from beginning to end

Ode to Tikkun V'Or

Spirit, Community, Justice at its core
What a shock to be in a pandemic
Kinda feels a little hallucinogenic!
This was a year of transition
We had high holidays in a church, our "mass" decision
We also said goodbye
To Rabbi Matzoh Bri
We had to adjust to platform Zoom
Which looked like the Brady Bunch squares in our room
During services some didn't know they weren't muted
And sometimes you could hear how they disputed!
Singing off key and trying to sing as one
Was indeed a special type of fun
It was so dissonant that it had a down home feel, kinda nice
All singing Hebrew with an extra spice
I must say of being on the Tikkun v'Or Board
It was a place where no one could afford to be bored
We had fearless leaders
That seemed to be mind readers
Kudos go out to Shira
Whose strength reminds of the Queen of the Gods, Hera
And a big shout out to heavy lifter Lauren Korfine
I salute them both with a virtual glass of Manischewitz wine
We are a smart, passionate and zany crew
And this is why I belong to THIS synagogue as a Jew

All I Ask

The virus in some states is a crime spree-ding
Some people do little to no impeding
All we ask
Is to wear a mask

Distancing social
Doesn't have to be so emotional
"If the president doesn't wear a mask I'm not either"
Or
"I don't like how with the mask I'm a heavy breather"
"It's an inconvenience, it's hot, I hate the look"
Hmmm. Do you know how many lives you just took?

Yes, people I've polled
Say the mask-wearing is getting old

If 95% of the population followed the CDC rules
We would save over 33,000 or so humans or jewels
Cuomo said, we do have in our power a way to be disease free
It's by following safe protocols, you as well as me

So, I hope you will join me, we're in this together
Even in the COVID19 pandemic weather
Stay home, remember, we are NY tough
Even when the going gets rough and we've had enough

Honestly, I believe Trump has always virtually
masked himself
WE know who he really is, let's shelf the orange elf

It's poetry time

Where I have to rhyme!
To make a poem one of a kind
And it's almost nine

It's partly a skill
Like climbing uphill
You know the drill
Giving me a l'il thrill

I wait
With a blank slate
The wheels are a churning
My thoughts are a burning

Topics are sometimes hard to get
I come up with some ideas I've never met
I have an audience tried and true
I surprise even myself with what I go through

I always come up with a poetic theme
Sometimes my words are encrypted, they aren't what they
seem
My poetry like my coffee: sometimes light, sometimes
dark
Who knows what next will start a spark?

Poem #7

"I hate Tennis" screamed the little boy
Throwing his racquet like it was a paltry toy
This hurts me so
Like a diplomatic row
But I know better
It is his fetter(..er)
That's what This is about
It's academic talk for cultural capital clout

It's really about his little body holding thousands of years
of hurt
It's because I'm a white woman now in concert
With his feelings and I try to get
His inner Trail of Tears, inner Columbus his Carlisle
School needs met
This is trauma
I was told NOT to get involved with the drama
But I teach tennis and feel some residual pain
They sometimes cry in frustration
I try to keep sane

But when it goes well, it goes oh so well!
They have fun, and dance with their racquets
as far as I can Tell

To the boys and girls that hate tennis
Some days I do too
Especially when I can't shake but shake the feeling blue

I said to the boy who hates tennis that that's ok, why don't
we play anyway? (and this worked!)

Tennis is a time to pause
It is our time to create our clause
The racquet strings symbolic of Wampum two row
I know by now where I don't go
It's probably the most challenging work i do at the Nation
But to have this mainly joyful experience,
I wouldn't trade it for any occasion

The Older, The Wild

Iris Apfel, the ninety some odd year-old fashion maven,
sustains my inner child
I've decided to take two courses
"History of Flameworking" through Corning Glass
Museum
and...hold your horses..
A non-credit course from Fashion Institute of Technology
"Vintage Shopping" made just for me
While some folks dress in Angel Heart and Flax
(that's cool I suppose, to wear these clothes)
I'm into fashion, so we all need to relax
My muses are Anna Sui and Alexander McQueen
Thinking back on my teenage modeling days, and what I
might have been
But no matter, I'm not quitting my job of the day
I still see literacy teaching as my way!
But I'm exploring different facets of my soul
Like my writing of poetry; I'm on a roll
Freedom of expression geniuses Sui and McQueen
Top designers that need to be "heard" and seen!
I understand high fashion is a form of rebelling
To the status quo, that's why they're selling
So maybe I'll wear one of my tulle skirts with combat
boots? (probably not)
Only blanks do I shoots!!!
For wearing designer clothes doesn't hurt anyone
It's actually perhaps to give a little jolt or perhaps stun
And OMG...also to have some fun!!!

For the fall semester

I have to fall sequester
Trying to figure out how to do face to face
It's July, and it feels like this option includes outer space
Probably at the Metro Center rooms will be capped at ten
I'm considering dividing my twenty into two tens then!
A three-hour class but giving each ten an hour and a half
Not sure if it makes sense or if I'm doing the correct math
Some of the instruction has to be on Zoom
Cause the secretary told me today there just isn't the room
(I hope I'll figure it out soon so it doesn't subsume)
I also have to learn Blackboard, our platform for the
college
I plan on getting help for this important knowledge
It's worrying me, it's kind of scary
We're nowhere near the endzone and I'm giving a Hail
Mary
All I can do is REALLY prepare
I feel like a juggler with lots of balls in the air
It's tough learning new things
Because sometimes it stings
Ready or not here I come
Hopefully in a month I won't feel so dumb

I taught English at twenty-four

British canon was what was in store
I chose <u>The Picture of Dorian Gray</u>
Oscar Wilde was punished for being gay
But that was not included in my lesson plan
It was all about the book rather than anything about the man
I also taught <u>A Tale of Two Cities</u>
Dickens work about the fall of the aristocracy's pretties
Again, I didn't initially talk much about the history
I found this literature for tenth graders to be a mystery
I looked young, had hair like Snow White
I wore unneeded glasses, and a uniform of suits; they
were my blight
Ricky and I did not get along
He called me the B word and others so strong
But there was one place he respected that was my turf
He was on the tennis team and he wanted a berth
I nonchalantly mentioned that he was playing well
After that he no longer put me through hell
Thirty some odd years later as I recall this fact
I wonder if he has children who in this way react
You never forget your first-year teaching
Some heavy lifting and far reaching
It was a challenge to keep my boat afloat
"If I could do some things over I would" she wrote

First Year Teaching at Oswego

My first year of teaching at Oswego was 2001
After the semester I wondered how I had done
I recall teaching a Practicum class
Maybe twenty students sitting en masse
Early into the semester something happened here
We were a mix of emotions, mostly fear
For September 11th occurred that day
I had to contact my students in the fray
We never really got over that event
Some had husbands in the military that could have
been sent
There was an environment not of happiness but dread
It didn't matter what I could say or what was said
So, my evals were awful, I felt ready to quit
But chairperson Pam and mentor Sharon wouldn't hear of it
Other classes I had done just fine
But my Practicum class! I started to whine!
Twenty years later, I'm ok, it is done
You always have the occasional class that doesn't gel,
that isn't fun
There was a member of the class, Joan, that sent me a
handwritten note
"You were a fine teacher" she wrote, I quote
I guess this seems a similar situation
When in 2001 I got my sorority initiation
I'm afraid COVID-19 will cover us like a blanket
From my experience I can almost bank it
But I'm older and wiser said she
I'll try my best in THIS circumstance, I'll just let it be

It's so beastly hot

Cool and level-headed, I'm not
I've changed my clothes three a time
Sweating buckets and flipped flopped feet grime
I walked to The Commons downtown
To the post office then I turned around
Ducked into Starbucks
For a vanilla sweet cream cold brew "deluxe"
We don't have central air
It's almost too much to bear
I'm sticky like rice
And my mood, well, I'm not completely nice
I know, I know, when it's cold I often complain
Which is worse? They both are a bane
Heat you can take off more stuff
And in your house you can be a "diamond in the rough"
We have air conditioning in the bedroom
So, we stay in there also to groom
I hope this poem explains it well
'Cause it feels like the bowels of hell

We lived in a modest home

But every spring my Dad wanted to roam
He was chief of pathology
And he felt his house went along with an apology
His associates lived in palatial homes on the Skaneateles
Lake
He didn't think he could anymore take
Every spring we would enter at least half dozen beautiful
big houses
Drunk with longing, my father carouses
The realtors felt the deal with the doctor was sealed
But no one told them they were out in left field
Once or twice he signed on the dotted line (and poof!)
He made my mother explain why this was no longer fine
I think my mom did a great acting job
She might have even broken into a sob
The contract was always null and void
The realtor would always mull on it and be annoyed
I loved our house on that lane in DeWitt
Why it caused my Dad pain he wouldn't really admit
He came from humble beginnings in Jackson Heights
Orthodox Jewish household and uncomfortable fights
He had gained recognition and a little fame
Dr. Kagan is his, and, also my name
His struggle with moving
Was because he had to be proving
That he was a big deal
Though maybe he didn't always feel
Like this for real

When you end a relationship

When you end a relationship after seventeen years
Of course, it is going to bring you to tears
For we enjoyed sports: tennis and football
And watching movies at the mall
We would go visit the family during holidays
It all is a bit of a haze
He and I loved our cats
I earned my doctorate with his congrats
Life happened, we went our separate ways
During that year I autopiloted my days
Then I met my second husband, at just the right time
He and I share a similar paradigm
Initially, I wanted someone so different from me
But that difference became so pronounced that I had to
let him be
Sometimes you have to go through pain
To ultimately make an irrevocable gain
I'm happy, older and somewhat more wise
I don't take things for granted, I now realize
I left it up to the match G-d and fate
And something happened, it is really great
For when one door closes another may open that feels right
It's easier to sleep at night

PBJ Almost Everyday

I eat peanut butter and jelly a lot
For lunch today, it seemed to hit the spot
Peter eats the more, savory fishy stuff
I like sweets and that awful stuff - fluff
Tonight, I was so frustrated I had a beer
My limit of one I fear
Peter doesn't have chocolate or booze
It's a choice that he chews
I'm downstairs surrounded by many a book
Peter's upstairs in his Peter nook
We typically get along very well
He the neatnik, me more of a "pell mell"
It's so nice not being alone
It's better than T.V. or phone
I have a live person and we understand
When we have to lend a helping hand
We're both battling technology in our "respective
academe"
He's winning I'm losing it DOES SEEM
But we're like peanut butter and fluff
It's a winning combo, this sweet stuff!

Netflix

I've been getting my kicks
By watching a lot of Netflix
We started watching when COVID hit
And now we're watching quite a bit
Peter doesn't own a T.V.
So, it's up to me
To curate the documentaries and sitcoms
From the winners, to the bombs
So, in our free time
At about nine
We sit on the couch
If it's later, I'm a grouch
We watch and laugh
Let's do the math
Two hours a night times seven days
Fourteen hours in the Netflix haze
We seem to love
When push comes to shove
Our little Isle of sofa red
And after we just fall in bed

Guns that Kill

My friend Rachel, and my friend Phil
- Are both writing about guns that kill
- Phil wrote a piece and it got national attention
- Rachel is finishing a book on guns religious fervor ascension
  - (You guys should talk)
- Three million more guns in the pipeline
  - Apocalypse is now a new byline
  - It's so scary, the threat is so real
- How can we take someone's temperature to see how they feel?
  - What if they're hopping mad that day
  - What if a lot of innocents are in the fray
    - It's total f%*(& ing madness
  - I have so much depression, sadness

My poem doesn't have any bullets left
I don't know, I feel bereft
We are losing our humanity
AND I'm using more profanity
Because this is the worldAF
I sure hope we are not shit out of luck

Very late morning

We went to Corning
A museum of glass
Wasn't crowded, no mass
We went to the hot shop
Front row, no one at the top
It was like the museum was for us
No lines, no fuss
The glass art exceeds expectations
No abominations
One time, a few years back I tried glassblowing
I burned my hand without knowing
I have a paperweight to show
To make up for my woe
I wish we could go beyond an hour away
But we really can't now, it's okay
I would love to travel
Unfortunately, the world did unravel
All those states that didn't follow simple rules
I think, "What fools!"
I guess we all live in our individual glass museum
Fragile, transparent, delicate as I see them
It's up to us to stay the course
We all know what to do…of course

CTFC

I belong to the Cornell Faculty Tennis Club or CFTC
In Ithaca, I agree
That it's the loveliest most beautiful outdoor place
You walk down to the bottom of the gorge, it is the space
Where we play tennis for hours at a time
The endorphins kick in, how sublime
The surface is a green-like clay
Sometimes the ball bounces funny, but mostly it's ok
I'm meeting new people, playing doubles
A cure for my "hybrid course" troubles
I play and I often am in the moment and forget
Then sometimes I'll hit an overhead in the net
But these aren't competitive games, they are fun
Wearing lots of 50 SPF 'cause we are in the hot sun
The feeling lasts for hours and hours
I wish it could last more with some magical powers
I love tennis
When I can finesse
It is my sport
I love holding court
Now if I can just consistently serve
It's a matter of nerve
I wish I could play tennis all day, every day
If I had my say, but my teaching gets in my way
I must balance, Oy Vay

Those Dirty Magazines....

Vogue and Bazaar
Magazines that are
Full of interesting fashion
Of which I feel a passion
Like high style Dolce Gabbana shoes
That make all the style news
I like to look at the high end
It's artwork adornment as I pretend…
My imagination
Brings consternation
I understand why some people this speaks of misogyny
That the women get the message o' skinny
But I think there is a movement – body positive – to
embrace
There are now models of different body types with a nice
face
I also hear that these mags are only for "young tarts"
Well, I also feel they are for the "young at hearts"
I talk to certain friends and I get a bizarre reaction
I guess I don't feel this has too much traction
I will keep on reading my In Style
For at least awhile
Yes, it is my vice
Other than this, I'm considered pretty nice

I'm a Hottie

I think I've just had a hot flash!
I'm pretty certain, I'll bet cash
I was just sitting in a chair
And I got stick to my neck hair
I'm wearing a sleeveless dress
And the heat is making a mess
This summer is way too hot
Comfortable I am not
So, I'm finally in menopause
That is the root and the cause
Of me feeling tremendous heat
All the way down to my feet
There's not much you can do for a remedy
I feel my body is the enemy
I hope I can just hang on
Without displaying a fang on
Cause my mate doesn't seem to understand
That I'm not in full command
Of my body
But I guess now you could say I'm a hottie

I just read on Face Book that My Close Friend Died

My close friend died
"Only forty-two!" I cried
He had such a beautiful voice
In his poems but at the end he had no choice
I feel like I've been punched in the gut
Knocked the wind right out of me, I'm in a rut
He taught poetry through Writer's Workshop at the
Native School
He dressed in Salvation Army rejects and was so darn cool
He and another poet had an amazing rapport
With the Native kids their sensitivity bore…
A respect…right to the core

He used to call me "Yenta" 'cause I gave (sometimes
unsolicited) advice
What did I know? But sadly, he paid a great price
He was in mourning, for the love of his life
A man who died suddenly, causing him so much strife
He never was the same
Inside his heart, it did maim

Years ago, I went to a gay bar in NYC called Mr. Black
I was with my posse who made sure I would make it back
Amy Winehouse singing about her rehab woes
The posse made sure I was correctly dressed from my
head to my toes
I'm still wearing the fateful Madonna tour tee
When I was with those guys, I felt so amazing, so free

I just don't feel like doing anything
I am so sad, I wish the phone would ring
And I would talk to my BFF and hear his signature laugh
He always timed it well, just after my gaffe
I'm so sorry, it leaves a space in my heart
Being with him was itself an art
Like when we went to The Met to see the designer magic
of Alexander McQueen
Through McQueen's dark lens his genius was to be felt as
well as seen
McQueen at forty-one, you at forty-two
My love, I just wish you were alive, and this weren't
actually true

Poem #136

I feel like I'm running out of things to say
This has caused me much dismay
This is poem number one-hundred and thirty-six
For some of you, it's your daily fix
I appreciate all the kind "atta girls"
It makes me feel wisdom among its pearls
But I'm not yet reading to throw in the towel
I still want to evoke humor, I want you to howl
So, I'm thinking of slowing down
When the semester starts so I don't drown
I am planning on having so much to do
To awaken I will have to drink plenty of cold brew
I hope you all understand
When I stop, I will be in command
Perhaps I will write two a week instead of seven
That may be for me a kind of heaven
So, I'll let you know well in advance
Of my pandemic poetry stance
I think some of them could reside in a l'il book
The ones that resonate, I'll have to take another look
So many poems with so many a topic
Many about the world but most a biopic
I'm telling you now as a barely audible warning
So I don't have to start my day by wondering in the
morning
Whether I will complete a poem by the end of the night
My poetic burden is being lifted and I feel kinda light

Ruth Bader Ginsburg, R.I.P.

I'm sitting downstairs
The shofar zooming upstairs
It's Rosh Hashanah, the New Year
A beginning to start and step into high gear
I didn't feel like going upstairs, was kind of sad
Something inside was just feeling bad...
And on the web, I just found out Ruth Ginsburg has died
She was our best Supreme Court justice and brilliant guide
I transformed into Ruth, in order to teach
How to dissent, how to reach
I wore my doctoral gown
Two necklaces to put around
One designating agreement, accord
The other dissent, disagree or "Oh Lord"
I read a picture book about her to squirming first graders
They loved the book and maybe they will grow up as
Ruth Baders
A little woman with a powerful intellectual prow-ess
I'll be a fan in memorandum I confess
There's no Truth without Ruth
For she was a sayer of "Sooth"
We have cup coasters here of her image
I'm hoping her granddaughter will continue her strong
law lineage
A role model, a heroine, and a mensch
The rock star, who sat for so many years on the bench
Ruth, so many of us have love
For you, now fighting for us...from above

Poem #2 on Notorious RBG

"I ask no favor for my sex. All I ask of our brethren is that
they take their feet off our necks"
This was a quote from Supreme Court Ruth
Who always spoke of her and our collective truth
But this has a whole new meaning
The neck we are speaking of is not a subject fleeting
In George Floyd
We have such a void
He kept saying, "I can't breathe"
The policeman overcome, started to seethe
Putting more and more pressure on his neck
For nine plus long minutes until George was a complete
wreck
The judge determining homicide
The public across the country divide and cried
For we have to stick out our necks
To protect our rights, against these roughnecks
We can't just sit and watch this go on
'Cause if we do we'll all be gone

My mother was a knitter

Always eye on the sweater prize she was no quitter
She would knit on her kitchen highchair
While talking on the phone, making a sweater of mohair

She made the greatest creations
She would knit my friends sweaters which were
sensations
She knit for a boutique on Newbery Street
That was an amazing, honorable feat!

I'd see her wear a surgical mask when working with mink
Also, some precious stones she added I think
I still have a sweater or two
But unfortunately, I grew and some more grew

I feel like carrying on the craft
But I would have to learn how to plan and draft
For you can't really improvise
And you have to have really wise eyes

She had a following and she taught
Women who were often fraught
They would say things like, "My arms are too wide"
It was not only about their knitting, but often what was
felt inside

Mon tended to these sickly sweaters
She cast off those imagined fetters

She was wise and could keep people in stitches
She spun tales that were abundantly delicious

Mom had knitted herself a career
I have my memory of that time-period clear
For she was the doyenne of her craft
Often giving her charges a brand new life raft

Bid(en)ing OUR TIME

The bells in foreign lands chime
For in January there will be a notable change
A needed power exchange
Hallelujah for Biden and Harris
News quickly got to Paris
World leaders are relieved
"Welcome Back America!" believed
So, we will soon start a new chapter
With a stark before and after
We have COVID to fight
This is a REAL plight
So, we will have a new prez and veep
Who will both roll up their sleeves and dig deep
Two birds of a feather
Working on bringing us together

Passover

My father never ever drank
Until every Passover, four glasses in the tank
He would reminisce about his childhood, and he told
corny jokes
While being chatty with all invited folks
Totally out of character from day to day life
Even grew affectionate, with my mother, his wife
Typically, Dad was Dr. Kagan, a rather serious man
But with those four glasses of wine, his mouth ran and
some more ran
Why did he wait for Passover to drink?
He posited "If it's in the Haggadah, one doesn't have to think."
I think he really saw Elijah when he got up to open the door
To him it wasn't just folklore, it became so much more
To lose himself, forget his cares
He drinks his wine and overshares
It was kind of funny, his drinking tradition
Always a repetition, each Passover, this covert mission

The Kagans

Grandpa Sol was always smiling
Notably charming, though "un"-beguiling
He wore a pair of hearing aids
My memory of his understanding now fades
Owned a garage in Jackson Heights
Turned off the "aids" during Grandma's fights
The whole Kagan family pilgrimaged to the Bar Mitzvah
of my big brother
In old Temple Adath Yeshurin, a beautiful place like no
other
I was four years old, but remember it well
Helping Mom prepare sandwiches, that captivating,
corned beef smell!
Mother was an outsider, according to "them" the corned
beef was on wry
Mocking her accent, they never truly accepted her;
I could sense it but then didn't know why
All uncles, cousins, aunts came to that event
It was all worth what my parents spent
The relatives decided fighting on this day would be
suspended
Though skirmishes and turf wars had not totally ended
Celebrating Jewish family in fine style galore
The event, totally worthwhile, and indelible at my age of
four

My mother, the goy or gentile from Switzerland

Grandma insulted her in Yiddish when she came to this land
My mother, a quick study in what grandma Molly was saying
Also, converted to be a Jew – Orthodox – by training
Mom acted so Jewish, no one believed she converted
When asked about Judaism she always answered and asserted
A very smart lady, she could be a chameleon with dialect
To various people she spoke with her phrasing decidedly select
Mom was never considered by grandma to be a Jew
Yet, my mom knew exactly what to do
Mom would say, "Oy Vay, be careful of the evil eye's glare."
And with no repartee, all grandma could do back was
gape and stare

Winter Soul-stice

It's the shortest day of the year
Winter solstice is finally here
Now is the winter of our discontent
With the COVID-19 this has meant
A dreary darkness has fallen, especially now
From naïve and careless gatherings, that is the how
How cruel is this disease
Making us feel completely ill at ease
~ We cannot trust each other
Strangers but also sister, brother and mother
Long nights
Interior fights
Darkness visible Styron deftly writes
Tricky thoughts that permeate
My fate
I decide to hold on instead of free fall
Our amber's waves of grain and my hope that G-d save
us, mostly all

What Unity Looks Like

Decorum has returned
This is FINALLY what we've earned
I heard Biden's speech today
Really listened to what he had to say
This is <u>exactly</u> what we now need
A strong message to take heed
So different is the tone. We, the US, have grown
I can now stand tall
With my physical and emotional wherewithal
Biden the beacon
Neither dividen' nor weaken
"My soul is in this" he said
For the last four years took its toll and we bled
UNITY, COVID IMMUNITY, MORE OPPORTUNITY,
REQUIRES INGENUITY
It may take a while to move forward again
But now there's hope, Love you Biden, Amen

It was fate.

Starting out as a Match.com date
We met at a small town bakery
There was no pretension or fakery
He stood at the counter barrier
And ordered our sandwiches definitively, like a Boston terrier
We ate while I was quite shy
But he was different, not my typical guy
We were both Jewish and professors
He was kind, unlike some Match aggressors
I'd dated a few professors but never one Jewish
Even though I was, so this was newish
We left and then continued on a hot chocolate quest
I kept thinking, "Wow. He's not like the rest."
I had stashed some Hannukah presents in my car, to
him, I confessed
He thanked me, smiled, and said, "I guess I passed the test."

"I'm having a birthday party tomorrow night."
I said I would try to come and thought I just might
I recall wearing a sweater pink
Just the right amount of demure I think
I got to his house
I was nervous and quiet as a mouse

By the booze I parked
"I like your sweater" an older woman remarked
We started talking and both had degrees in Special Ed.
Her Brooklyn brogue gave her street cred

Forty-five minutes later he looked at me across the
room with dread
I walked over to him. "Is there something wrong?" I said
"That's my mother" he turned a shade of red
"Oy Vay" I muttered
My heart fluttered

I knew more about his mother
Than I did any other

Flash forward six years
A Jewish wedding complete with joyful tears
For what if I didn't give him the Hannukah presents that
were in my car?
What if I didn't talk to his mom at the makeshift bar?
That magical Hannukah weekend I will remember always
It was the "oil" that sealed our relationship in many ways

The history of us gets replayed every year
We go to the place of our first date with cheer
The first light of love in the bakery we found
It lasted a lot longer, struck by a match, and now is sound

Dancing at Trader Joe's

Trader Joe's
Has stopped my woes
While I'm on my toes
I found myself DANCING in the frozen aisle
To the song "Call me Maybe" DISCO style
Alongside the frozen peas
I swiveled my hips and unlocked my knees,
Peter, there, saying "That's my wife."
Shoppers staring while I run rife!
The in-store music is danceable and upbeat,
I'm sure they field test the songs, so you'll buy more meat,
It all boils down to marketing
That is why we're harkening!
Prancing among brussel sprouts I wouldn't trade,
an Average Joe experience for the shopping frolic that I made!

It's Time

Memories of a relationship gone astray
Hit like bullets, a PSTD way
The grooves were getting deeper
Before I was saved by my forever keeper
Rebirth happens, comes at a cost
What was there, is what is lost
The Age of Innocence, my favorite book
May Welland, her world completely shook
Time answers the mysteries
Of past searing histories
But to get beyond, you have to dig deep
And learn, for What you sow is what you reap

The Life of Jenny

On summer solstice, I was born
It was Father's Day, early in the morn
A lamp he bought me instead of a stuffed bear
Symbolizing that I was the light of his life
And this was something rare
I grew up, parents very protective
Until I took the adolescence elective
I paid the price in blood
That's how my memories flood
Now that I've learned to love again
It was all a matter of when
A perfect match was found
He had to scrape me off the ground
The memory of that day, will not go away
But time heals the wounded
Soldiering on
Hopefully you'll get this message before it's gone

Poem #68659

Undercover humanity spies
It's in the eyes
But Why's? (I dunno, search me)
Listening to real punk The Clash
Who Rock the Casbah with their jet fighters stash
Feel my energy, going to the troops
But Alas, I'm crazy, total fruit loops!
So, I sing and dance with no audience anymore
Not like when I was nineteen, a budding woman for sure
BUT this bud was for you!
Never thinking it would be interpreted as a beer can, on
the ground, discarded.

Poem #582

Some People (not ALL) who are soley organic
Are sometimes people in an existential panic
Social JUSTICE via only yoga and meditation
Doesn't have such variation
Elitism, I See You Ivy Leaguer
You leave me well, completely beleagured!
For it's THE DOING not the food or enlightenment for
selfish purpose
Trust me, it will ALL KARMA surface.
Or bending like a pretzel, dog or cat/cow
It is more about the REAL Power of NOW
But for you it's a cage free guise
Look me straight in the eyes
Sorry for my lack of eye contact that you think are lies.
For some not ALL: Do you want that veggie burger with
fries?

Poem #295

Written on Memorial Day
I'm in a Memorial space...
The Earth is a wise place
It makes choices
Depending on the voices

Sending love to our troops
Although, I'm a PACIFIST...Whoops!
They fight for our rights
In the middle of the nights
Defending the US
And how we got in this mess...

It's not a competition or game
We are all the basically the same
We start out as Good Eggs
Then we make choices the question begs

We stand upon our flesh and blood, our DNA?

This makes us who we are today
Maybe I'm just a little bit cray cray???

My Latent Adolescence

Mascot for boy's lacrosse team
Playing for them a deferred dream
Ready to be first EVER girl to play
Dad wouldn't sign medical, contact sport, no way!
A sort of '80's androgenous he, she…she, he
A budding psychologist. A Yoda, grasshoppaa from
Kung-Fu, but JUST me
Friendly to All
Always Dancing, singing, a living, breathing…doll
THEN
 Puberty hit, maybe, sixteen?
Unbalanced on the balance beam
Gained a serious fifteen
Pounds of woman but as strategy decided to starve my hips
107 lbs on Sherriff's ID card, but it turned out, shit, that I
was sinking even more ships.
So, then I learned about the other more mature lacrosse
games that I had a hard time playing. Was watching from
the sidelines, cheering,
I'm JUST saying
NEVER have I tried to steal a committed heart
Or had a part
In the undoing of a relationship.
That's not my scene
Cause, I'M friendly, definitely not at all mean

The Growth Mindset

This Associate Professor would like to lecture you
On the growth mindset...looks like a different hue!
When your mindset is fixed
Life feels like it's playing tricks!

Growth means you focus on the process
This is the key to healthy success

Fixed, you may be threatened by the success of others
Be it your mom's, friend's or sister and brothers

Fixed can lead to CHEATING or even DECEPTION
Naw, Growth mindset focuses on rapt and loving
attention

I was a late bloomer, small in a big world
I just sat on the sidelines while life unfurled

Now, I'm in the driver's seat full of love (and a little pain)
But I know in my heart, where I'll never go again!

To Write Moving Poems

To write moving poems
One must be careful when dipping into the well
Of the unconscious

Make sure you come out whole again
To maintain your beautiful soul and then

Rest, relax, give in to sleep!

Do your best to keep
Your hard-fought sanity
With a dab of empathetic humanity

Onyx, Ebony...

Shiny, bright
Loved animals
Superhero costumes worn to attract...
Attention
People were always staring, blown away at his
impeccable beauty
While I was wearing a heavy burka, walking ten paces
behind
Problems of the heart
99.9% blockage
Saved him but
The story unravels in the man cave
His choice: wandering the Earth then marrying Kryptonite

New beginnings
Now with a love/friend
who wears shirts from Kohl's that I help pick out
and seems better suited
for me
has less heart issues
semi-vegan BFF
Things seem to be getting better...
Commitment
Shed burka: new fashion sense and unique style
Thank you

Ho Hum Dumb Dee Dumb

Many poets before me have written about the sacred in
the mundane
(I guess that is the essence of poetry)
That's cool!
Ho Hum Dumb Dee Dumb
But poetry has to be very cryptic?
Not totally understood to be published?
Ho Hum Dumb Dee Dumb
I am NOT published; and I guess people have said my
poems need to be:
Workshopped
I need to be in an M.F.A. program
I write like "Shel Silverstein"
(I love Shel Silverstein)
Ho Hum Dumb Dee Dumb
When I get a heart emoji from one of my fans
I light up like a Christmas tree (or in my case a menorah)
Ho Hum Dumb Dee Dumb
I never expected to enroll in a virtual Life 101 class when I
write my poems
A self-paced course that I take with sometimes a few
surprises
But I seem to take it…in stride
Ho Hum Dumb Dee Dumb

Red Ribbon Redux

Recall my other poem: When I was born the nurses put a
red ribbon in my hair and said knowingly, you have "that
one"
Well, the mystery is...kind of done
I'm a freestyle baby
Who dances in Trader Joes to "Call me Maybe"
Who flew on the Omega trapeze
Spirit soaring...if you please!
Just try to define me and I'll change
Try to malign me and I'll act strange
I believe the United States wants people with United
States
Cast off those invisible shackles and sing
Home on the Range, Vogue, Billie Jean...
ANYTHING!!!!!!!!!
Cracking up my BFF secretar...ee
When moving offices I put a mailing label on me!
Oy Vay, what is this world about????
Makes me want to vamp and pout (too old, psyche!)
Watching YouTube Janet and Michael dance
Eyeing their freestyle moves gives me rhythm and a
chance
If life's To Be or Not to Be
Let's be free mother.....kas, free free freefree

Tuesday of Birthday Week

The fog has lifted
"I AM GIFTED" ho hum, Ommmmm
Who the hell cares?
Climb those stairs!!!
We all are in some way,
At our BIRTHday

My momma said we all possess a toilet brush (huh?)
"Ours is royal lavender and more plush"
For the more gifted the more we have to do the work!
That's a…perk?
Anyway.
There's sooo many gifted out there!
Dizzy Gillespie, Yo Yo Ma, Fred Astaire

UNDERSTAND that you're a star
Be HAPPY with who you are
Kindness wins the game
…On my racquet frame
"Dares dat dame"
The Tennis Lady, in the personal Hall of Fame

Wednesday of Birthday Week!

Last night's trip to Wegmans ~ lots of revision decisions!

Dressed in a Cape Cod vibing, Annie Hall type dress,
brown with white stripes with specs and a straw hat
I needed to go to Wegman's ~ cause that's "where it was
at"
For I have to eat
Even when I feel beat
I step to the beat of my own drum
Deliberate, strong, "Fe Fi Foe Fum" words of an English
mum
I pass the Enlightenment ice cream bars (and say to
myself…marketing)
Looking for Swiss chocolate from the Mars company
(harkening)

Go to get Almond Silk
Hearing twangy country music in back, behind the milk
OY, What is happening here?
Can judgment day be near? (nah it's just country music)

In six days, I will be fifty-seven!!
Wiser, sober, mindful…is this heaven? (hmmm. not
exactly…)
I skip lightly towards the blueberries, raspberries and
strawberries, mute
I pick the ones that are the most beaut

Thoughts go to...How can we SEVENTY MILLION hate?
Seriously. It's time to concentrate
On our fate

Oy Vay, What have we done?
Oy Vay, What have we become?
Who did this?
How did we let him...our abyss?

I try to take the WORLD CLASS view
Like Fed, Swiss, American, and a Jew

Alienated from this "survival of the fittest" world
The "cult of humanity" nature has unfurled

Livin' on street smarts, brown sugar pop tarts, "I'm so
tough"
Like a hugger mugger jelly filled donut, red rose, panda/
polar bear (hybrid) rough (I kill...mosquitos)
I've taken a different tone of late
Battling and refuse to hate
I've established a fighting weight
To abate
The blue team/red team debate

RED is for Switzerland, Valentine's Day, love
BLUE is for damask, toile, the skies above
How do we love? DOVE! (bars in aisle 12!)

We're in this together
In any kind of weather

I wish, "G-d. Wouldn't it be great to be in Switzerland?"
but this is the US
I hope for our collective Olympic best! Go Team USA!!!!
I will not rest
Until we get As on our test
And rebuilt our nest
Let's get back to our BEST

Thursday of Birthday Week

Close Encounters
At nineteen, I'm in the hospital, prostrate
Goodness, I've lost a ton of weight

Arms outstretched
Eyes rolling towards the sky
Holding me down, a man cries…why?

Having an "adverse reaction to medication"
But perhaps it's the archetypes in one's meditation
Greek, mythology, Catholic, Jew
It's in my DNA, but it's also in YOU

An East Indian nurse
Looks at me with beautiful brown eyes
She looks at my diminutive size

Is present, she gives me a gift
She touches my forehead, where there's a rift

Anointing me with the third eye dot
The kind gesture meant such, a lot
Can't admit this to many
Though Mom would say, "Oh, That's my Jenny"

Now the tennis world calls me The Tennis Lady and Ja Chill
I strive to do my personal best, rather than run of the mill
I take children's Benadryl

Now to guide me to sleep
For today's world, just has me weep

I have bruises and mysterious contusions
I don't think they're delusions or confusions

I live by the metaphor of the ballerina dancing, broken leg
Basically, it's really tough to be a VERY good egg

Juneteenth

Proclamation
Of race relations
Consolations
Integration
Verification
Of revelations
Acclamation
World salvation
Vibrations
Stimulation
Confirmation to the peace of the world
Stevie Wonder's brilliant lyrics from "Song in the Key of
Life" ~ Pastime Paradise
He was soooo wise!
This proud morning of Juneteenth Federal Holiday
Let's make way
For honoring our ~ brethren
Having to follow that big dipper towards Heaveren
People like Michelle Obama
 Is the Obama!
That makes us celebrate OUR Becoming
Beautiful, vivacious, yes, pretty stunning
Personally, I have my Arrington fam
That grounds me in who I am
Whenever I get bleary eyed or mystified
I reach out to my African-American sis's
The righteous Misses and Mrs.
Music to the 'Cuse Elementary School King

Amazing Ithaca College music teachers praises I sing.
So happy! Together I did bring!
For remember when "they go low we go high"
That's when The Limit is the sky!

Father's Day

I swam under water
To pick up my Fater
who was drowning
We resurfaced
both gasped for air
luckily when we were out of "there"

Initially, I didn't understand and thought the attention
Was too much to mention
But mom told me that the original plan of the red
ribboned little girl
Was to save his life

For in HIS NUCLEAR family
There was too much strife

He taught me because you are in the Cohen/Kagan tribe
You have a role that you have to keep alive
Dr. Kagan, my father a physician,
Making weighty decisions
Me, Dr. Kagan, an associate professor/manager: May I
help you please
I teach at Oswego State, while he cured disease
"I will be your father figure
Put your tiny hand in mine
I will be the one that loves you
Till the end of time" ~ George Michael

My husband reminds me
Of our family tree
Jewish, family oriented, loves order and the lawn
It's like I'm back in a way, on me it suddenly dawns
That who I married was Chosen, by mom, by you
My grandma interrupting (of course), saying, "Catsela...
Oy. So, Nu?"

Birthday Poem

I'm reading Michelle Obama's memoir
And Indigenous Crazy, Brave by Joy (Harjo)
Well, Hello!
And Allen Ginsberg's disturbing Howls
Three distinct voices, I dig deep with my own personal
gardening trowels
Deeply moved by their words
My mind goes to reincarnation?
Nature wants a do-over? ~ Maybe that's what we need as
a nation
Or maybe JUST do the work!
Turn off the TV station
Work hard at your vocation
Go about your "zen" integration
Don't let others undermine your balance
Maintain your valiance
Do not be disturbed
Or perturbed
Advice I should take; I turned fifty seven today
I'm a little gray
I took a two-and-a-half hour hike today
It felt so good
To be in the wood
I finally felt understood
As the little engine that could…

Caregivers

With dis-ease
It's difficult being the spouse
Bearing witness to the machinations
Trying to set right the somewhat…lucid hallucinations
Setting limits on time, boundaries
So that you don't also catch the dis-ease

For I don't want our innocence tainted
With pictures that have been previously painted

Going on walks
Trying to some sense talk
Traveling down memory lane
Little York pond makes me sane
Sedated (sometimes I feel)
Proud boy baited
Mine eyes have seen the glory…
But that's ANOTHER movie, story
Trying to maintain composure
After exposure
All anyone can do is laugh, cry
Make music, don't ask why
Go about your business and live parallel to normal
Don't be formal
Talk to friends, get support
Join groups that proport
Life's for the living
Care taking, care giving

Heidi the Mighty

Friends since we were one years old
Over fifty-five years, able to talk, in friend code
You're an artist, I'm like your kid sistery
You guide me through many a life's mystery (like
Venmo…ha)
Heidi is an anthropologist extraordinaire and
Anthropologie is her style
Hey, it's not harming anyone, and it makes us both smile!
Heidi studies different aspects of the human experience
And is an artist with influence and reappearance
Sense of color, expertise in design
Having a long partnership with Rosita…Fine
Necklaces are her new gig!
Love 'em, on Etsy, I hope they're gonna be big
Paintings of the fabric of our lives
Into the core she deep dives
For aren't we basically performance art?
With some, or in this case a lotta heart?
Like actors, our wardrobe allows us to take on different
parts
This is how we reveal our smarts
Some of us, like to push the envelope and are "off the
charts."

I hear of promising kids

I hear of promising kids
And then to find out the disease hids
Comes on at nineteen or twenty
The shift is more than a plenty
You are someone's cherished daughter or son
So brilliant, you should have won!
Sad the fates got in the way and dealt you a rough hand
I know, now you feel you're on foreign land
For when it strikes it bids farewell
And opens up the gates of well, an inner hell
To navigate you need meds, therapy and rest
To get you back to where you're best
You may feel a tad sedated
Know that no one feels you're hated
But don't go down the road of 'cide
Your thoughts irrational, they have to you lied
Stay strong you're resilient, more that you know
Try to tune out the inner, taxing, foe
You're a child of G-d, loved you are
This mantra may take you (say it to yourself!) far
For now I teach at a higher learning institution
Life is good (I'm fifty-seven) no need for any retribution
I make a salary and am brave
I act a little odd, kooky but mostly I behave
I know you can do this with the right combinations
No one's to blame, it's mainly genetic causations
I tell this to the anointed, the special, ok the brilliant, the few
Whatever it takes (and it will take) try to be back to YOU

Last Night in Whalen

Last night we traveled to Whalen
Where the sounds were absolutely wailin'
And it was smooth sailin'!

I always get choked up
When in the audience I see many a young pup
The campers grooving to the beats
Of their idols no small feats

The music faculty at Ithaca College
Impart by example their hard won knowledge
In such beautiful ways
The young audience grooves and sways

Then the high schoolers adamantly cheer
Because of what they hear
I'm a prof at another school
And my students don't think I'm THIS cool

Oh, each of you is a rock star
Through their eyes that's what you are
You raise the bar
With love, far but not THAT far

I'm Odd, Thank G-d

I was told "You're a little odd"
Said my student with a little nod
So what's my rebuttal
About this scuttle?

I'm still mental age twenty-five
Still have movement and a bit of jive
Still "Stayin' Alive"
With the youthful drive, I thrive

I don't really worry anymore
About Jen Kagan folklore
To me it's such a bore
 Doesn't bother, I'm not taking score!

It's a reaction
From a faction
Of naysayers brought into the fray
And to this I say…
"The dichotomy of you and me is…gray"

Because creativity is my strength
I'll go to a great length
Of thinking outside the box
Will bagel earrings and a side of lox

I often carry a phone purse
For better or for worse
It has a stealthy function
It's a conversation junction!

I put on my uniform day
Like a soldier of fashion
If I may
I have a style vacation and I float but I stay

So those who think I am odd
I roll my eyes and say "Thank G-d".
For it is really odd to say that to your professor
You, the boundary-less confessor!!!

CPSIA information can be obtained
at www.ICGtesting.com
Printed in the USA
LVHW090409110222
710655LV00005B/582

9 781977 245960